Reptile World

Coral Snakes

by Imogen Kingsley

Bullfrog Books

Ideas for Parents and Teachers

Bullfrog Books let children practice reading informational text at the earliest reading levels. Repetition, familiar words, and photo labels support early readers.

Before Reading

• Discuss the cover photo. What does it tell them?

• Look at the picture glossary together. Read and discuss the words.

Read the Book

• "Walk" through the book and look at the photos. Let the child ask questions. Point out the photo labels.

• Read the book to the child, or have him or her read independently.

After Reading

• Prompt the child to think more. Ask: Coral snakes are venomous. What other snakes can you think of that are venomous?

Bullfrog Books are published by Jump!
5357 Penn Avenue South
Minneapolis, MN 55419
www.jumplibrary.com

Library of Congress Cataloging-in-Publication Data

Names: Kingsley, Imogen, author.
Title: Coral snakes / by Imogen Kingsley.
Other titles: Bullfrog books. Reptile world.
Description: Minneapolis, MN: Jump!, Inc., [2017]
Series: Reptile world
"Bullfrog Books are published by Jump!"
Audience: Ages 5-8. | Audience: K to grade 3.
Includes index. Identifiers: LCCN 2016050860 (print)
LCCN 2016051580 (ebook)
LCCN 2016051580 (ebook)
ISBN 9781620316658 (hard cover: alk. paper)
ISBN 9781624965425 (e-book)
Subjects: LCSH: Coral snakes—Juvenile literature.
Classification: LCC QL666.O64 K5625 2017 (print)
LCC QL666.O64 (ebook) | DDC 597.96/44-—dc23
LC record available at https://lccn.loc.gov/2016050860

Editor: Kirsten Chang
Book Designer: Molly Ballanger
Photo Researcher: Kirsten Chang

Photo Credits: Paul Marcellini/Getty, cover, 3; Don Filipiak, 1; Larry Ditto/Photoshot, 4, 14–15; Joe McDonald/Photoshot, 5; 1125089601/Shutterstock, 6–7; Snowleopard1/iStock, 8–9; Noah Fields, 10–11; Eric Isselee/Shutterstock, 12; Michael & Patricia Fogden/Getty, 13; Dr Morley Read/Shutterstock, 14–15; fivespots/Shutterstock, 16; Deatonphotos/Shutterstock, 17; Michael & Patricia Fogden/SuperStock, 18–19; John Cancalosi/Getty, 20–21; Seth Patterson/Getty, 22; Joe McDonald/Shutterstock, 23br; Joel Sartore/Getty, 24.

Printed in the United States of America at Corporate Graphics in North Mankato, Minnesota.

Table of Contents

A Shy Snake

What is in the leaves?

It is a coral snake.

She is shy.

She likes to hide.

She has stripes.

Red, yellow,
black, yellow.

They are bright.

They warn animals.

Stay away!

head

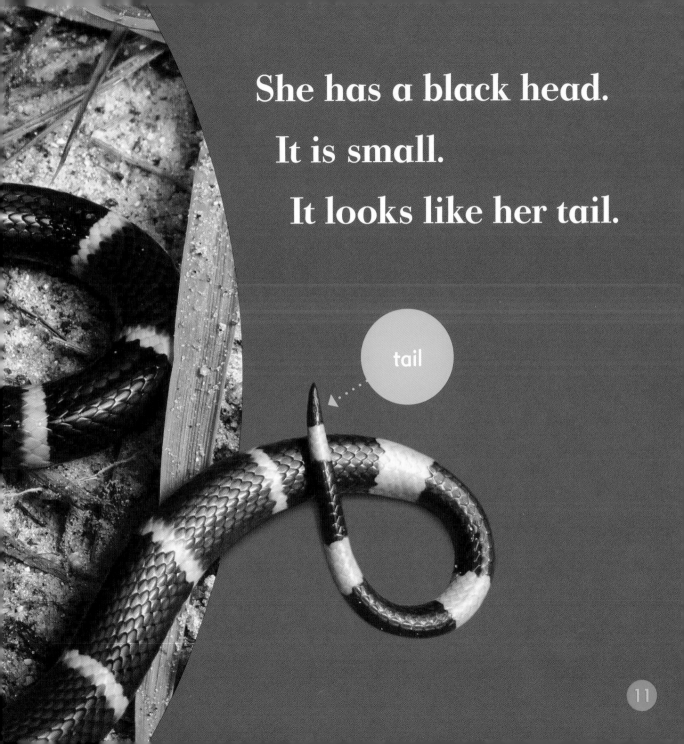

She has a black head.

It is small.

It looks like her tail.

tail

She lays eggs
in the summer.

egg

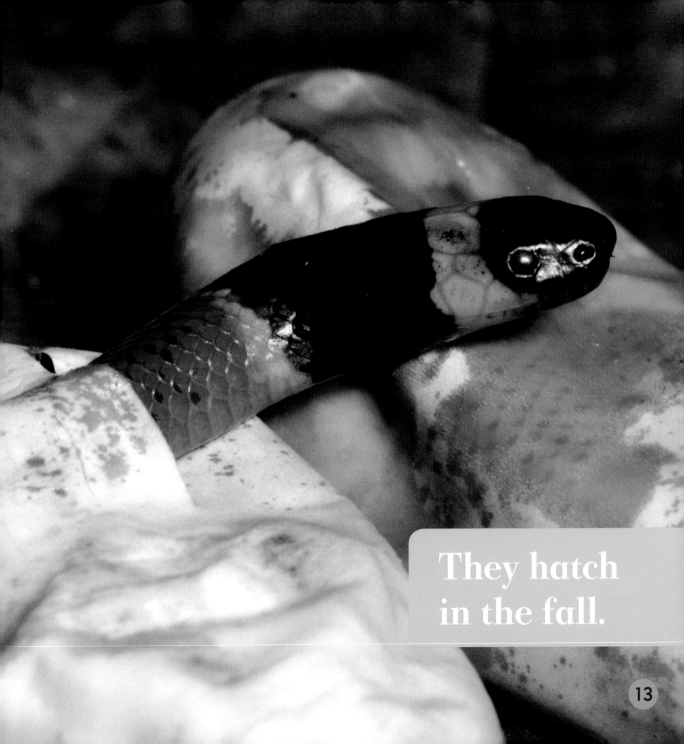

**They hatch
in the fall.**

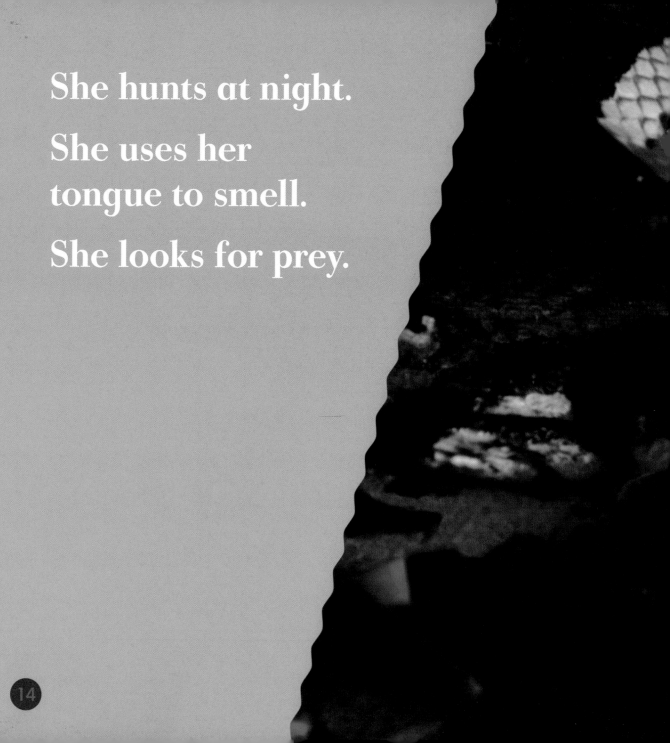

She hunts at night.

She uses her tongue to smell.

She looks for prey.

tongue

She eats lizards.

She eats frogs.

She eats snakes, too.

She bites.

Venom comes out
of her fangs.

The prey dies.

She eats.

Then she sleeps.

Parts of a Coral Snake

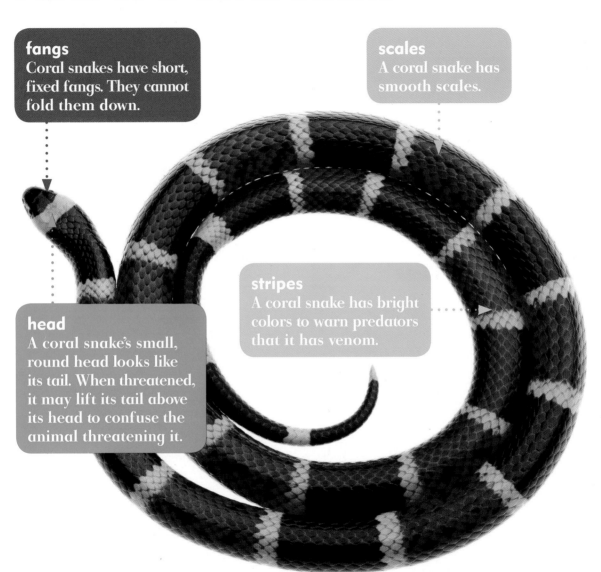

fangs
Coral snakes have short, fixed fangs. They cannot fold them down.

scales
A coral snake has smooth scales.

stripes
A coral snake has bright colors to warn predators that it has venom.

head
A coral snake's small, round head looks like its tail. When threatened, it may lift its tail above its head to confuse the animal threatening it.

Picture Glossary

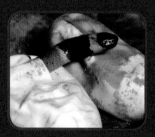

hatch
To be born
out of an egg.

prey
Animals that
another animal
hunts and eats.

lizards
Reptiles with
four legs
and a tail.

venom
Liquid poison.

Index

To Learn More

Learning more is as easy as 1, 2, 3.

1) Go to www.factsurfer.com

2) Enter "coralsnakes" into the search box.

3) Click the "Surf" button to see a list of websites.

With factsurfer.com, finding more information is just a click away.